A bridge flies away through a wild mist…
O, if only the river of floating peach petals
Might lead me at last to the mythical cave.
~Chang Hsu

We live in grief and ecstasy.
It is our justice.
~Gerald Stern

THE OUTSKIRTS OF KARMA

Poems by Alfred Encarnacion

Illustrations by Hong Xia

THE OUTSKIRTS OF KARMA

Poems by Alfred Encarnacion

Illustrations by Hong Xia

i

First published by Aquinas & Krone Publishing, LLC 2/16/2012.

ISBN # 978-0-9849505-0-8

This book is printed on acid-free paper.

Cover design by Tim Litostansky.
Edited by Judith Kristen.

In memory of Martha Quigley (1918-1993) and
Stephanie P. Quigley (1953-2001)
the two Bertha Taylors, Mary and Andy Sullivan
"When the moon shines bright…"

And for Lilyan Encarnacion, Paris Colello,
and Ginger Osment
"Keep on shining"

Thank you Hong Xia, artist extraordinaire,
for embracing my vision;
Judy, Andrew, and Tim at Aquinas & Krone for
believing in this book;
Phil Terman, Chris Bursk, Richard St. John, and
Denise Duhamel for your friendship

Contents

Marginalia

Sometimes my life seems scribbled
in someone else's marginalia.

I read the *I Ching* to be enlightened
but nothing changes; I read it

for pure entertainment & suddenly
it's prophetic as the TV Guide.

I will pack the dark bags of sorrow
under my eyes, follow the river

This poem almost
connects the new
and the ancient

curves to a hut on the outskirts of
Karma, wait in lotus position

for Buddha's call on my cellular phone.
I will sing as the roof

of nipa leaves bursts into flames
& wind blows away

my name like smoke from a shadow
set on fire.

Song
(with a line from Mary Oliver)

Joy's alive, sings the cardinal
one day in the spring,

in his throat her half-brother,
Hope, twists like a worm

She's alive, dance the bees,
swarming ballet of mimes

The trees lift their arms,
the porch sinks

in roses, daylilies,
the music of wind chimes...

What haunts us is absence
In the family of things

Joy's the lost child,
the one kidnapers steal

for fabulous ransom,
the one we spend lifetimes

The thyme
Scheme makes
this poem
More engaging

2

trying to buy back
The voice of the mother,

bruised with regret,
rises from childhood

Pay with your sorrows,
your coffers of tears,

she whispers High in the pine
tree, in its artery of branches,

radiant with sunlight,
the hive fills with honey

Sorrows

They may be worth something someday,
don't discard them too quickly

Like many things they prove
harmful only in excess

Given the right imagination
they convert into capital

I like the economic metaphors

Wisely invested
they yield high dividends

Store them in a safe place
until sure of their value

Trade them with temperance
taking advantage of no one

Understand it's their sharing
that can rescue the bankrupt

Beware of anyone who hoards them
or throws them away

Gravity

Gravity never betrays us,
never falls asleep on the job,
holds us always in a secret

embrace. On luminous wings
we soar to the sun,
our bodies made of honey & wax.

beautiful imagery

How soon we fall back into the world
like rain! Gravity
tugs at our slippery heels

says, *Do me a favor,*
keep one foot on the earth. Slowly
we learn to find happiness

in the weight of all things.
When death dons a tuxedo,
spins his dark wheel

& whispers our number,
gravity is the last
to let go of our hands.

Closing both eyes
we relinquish each thought
& float out of our bodies

weightless as breath

August

Tonight the wind moves slowly.

You can hear its song through the cornfield,
watch the stalks swaying in moonlight.

One day the sky will remember to snow
and the creek turn to ice in its bed.

But August is the kingdom of plenty.
The wolf in each worm may howl--

the tall ears of corn hear nothing.

This is too short, but the
illustration aids the words.

Deserted Village, Endless Mountains

They are gone. What remains of them is a presence that hovers
above our heads like a pale moon haunting the morning sky.
All afternoon we explore dark musty houses, the remnant
of a chapel--half its gray roof flown away in some storm--
a graveyard overrun with thickets so dense we stumble
over names carved deep in worn markers. Far below us
the valley is pine; a thread of brightness, its river runs south;
west of here hawks circle mauve peaks in the sun.
Whatever's abandoned the land will reclaim. These silent
dirt streets belong to lichen and ragweed. Stray dogs follow
us shyly, pretending they're wolves. Under its breath
the wilderness whispers. We listen like mice, feel more
than the eyes of owls upon us. When we drive away
at dusk, sounds of wind carry down the mountain
for miles like the villagers calling each other by name.

There is an overwhelming sense of
familiarity to this, especially in the latter
portion.

Plane Passing Above a Cow Pasture

Idle, at peace, they stand gazing intently at nothing,
or bowing their heads graze content on the slopes
of this sinking day. At sunset, the jet, avid for arrival,
smears a shadow across the land, where it falls
grass instantly darkens crumbling to ash
and the cows, one by one, are changed to stone.

I like the effect of the shadow
maybe we all turn to stone
under the cover of shadows

Express

Out of nowhere,
sudden as thunder,
it comes torpedoing
across night's
clear stillness.
Its blue light sizzles
over the fields,
the trees & scattered
houses. Blazing
by, half-luminous
with speed, prodigy
of power whose
soul's an incantation
of diesels.
Space opens
& closes behind
it like water.
Departing, its wake
glimmers briefly
in a backwash
of silence.

my father drove
trains for 25 years
this reminds me of him.
there is a allusion
to the old transcontinental
railroad and the "wild west"

The Green Man Comes to Bucks County
(in memory of John Haines
who read at Founders Hall, 1985)

He stood like a birch
barely moving on stage.
I saw no birds cling to his limbs,
not one nest in his ear.
If wind roared through that brain
it made only a wave
mildly rippling his hair.
Eyes blinded by April--
glasses corrected. I never leaned close
to attest to his breath--whether redolent
of roses--and whatever maggot
once sang in his beard
was lost when he shaved.
Only his boots seemed to be
as he said: old and discolored,
full of the memory of red mud
and dung, as though he'd walked here
through wild green valleys,
perhaps led by stray dogs,
to bring us these words--
quiet, exalted--
like a fresh fall of rain.

[handwritten annotation:] some odd word choices for an "In memory" piece use of maggots and dung perhaps this man was working class, but he spoke with eloquence

11

"Autumn: Hounds, Game, Fruit and Vegetables"
Alexandre-Francois Desportes, c.1712

Two hounds--one slyly
crouching to lap the hare's
warm blood,
the other snarling
to guard his master's
spoils--contend
on either side
of the rich brown pelt
flung upon the piled
squash and celery, greens
gathered from the fields,
potpourri of clustered grapes,
plums that shimmer
in tight skins,
the rosy cheeks
of peaches
polished in the sun.
But terror burns
in the dead hare's eye,
staring out of history:

reminds me of the vinyards in chile the sprawling fields of fruit (grapes)

12

death at the heart
of harvest, blood
before the feast.
A careful hand
has hung the pheasants
upside down,
nailed them like decrees
to the thick bark
of a tree. One feather
falls through centuries…

The Snake Plant

It's learned to keep secret
  and survive these days
  of cool winter light.

Out of the red planter
  the green appendages rise--
  some gnarled, some broken--

[handwritten annotation: reminds me of a book I used to read as a child, especially with the image of the window sill]

committed to their own agenda.
  It must dream of summer:
  the delicate vines of the

asparagus fern, stretching
  clean as memory, and everywhere
  the whine of cicadas

issuing from shrill,
  translucent husks.
  How private it sings, locked

in its own history, how
  mysterious and striking
  like a nest of cobras.

goodnight moon!

Modern Love

Another love story hits
  the morning papers.

Another mother's daughter
  raped and mutilated,

her body left to bleed out
in a trash bag at the dump.

*all too common
a situation in
_ Philadelphia
where I'm from*

Another father's son furious-
ly scrubs blood from his hands,

from his mind, midnight's sickle
moon a metaphor for his rage.

Commuters turn their pages.
The train streaks across the bridge.

Above the river, wheeling gulls
  circle our darkest headlines,

*Why is it
called modern
love, is it meant
to be ironic*

the sky filled with perfect
  spirals of flight.

On the 413

someone's pulled a gun,
    taken our driver hostage.
        Sirens. Squad cars flashing
in the rain. SWAT teams
    maneuvering in...
        We stare silent
as fish trapped inside
    an aquarium.
        The thin black
girl opens her umbrella,
    positions it like a shield.
        (In danger, the puffer
inflates up to twice
    its ordinary size--body
        language that says:
Don't fuck with me!)
    First shot goes off.
        We drop to the floor.
Thrashing.
    Helpless.
        Fish out of water.

[handwritten annotation:] is this a true story it's crazy he's thinking up a poem in that moment, but I guess those images never would vacate your mind

At the House of Chen

The prudent waitress asks
if everything's okay.

But life gets weirder
all the time. Lately

when you close
your eyes you imagine
people stop—frozen
in their tracks—

till you lift your lids again.

Sometimes it's startling
to believe how dead
you'll be one day;

even now you're just
a lively corpse
sharing the duck sauce,

the dim sum (God,
chicken feet!), afraid ⅂– lol

to end this meal, afraid
of screams inside
your pores. You close

your eyes so tight,
so very, very tight.

Identifies the fears we all have
of death. The thought of how
dead you will be some day rings so
true, most of US will be forgotten.

In the Hall of the King of the Terrible Lizards

(Tyrannosaurus Rex,
Philadelphia Academy of Natural Sciences)

He stands
on stupendous bird claws--
mogul of bones,
prehistoric yokel--
hopelessly gawking.
The walls rise:
muraled marshland
filled with hisses,
malevolent vines,
ferns cumbersome
as behemoths
feasting on tender
foliage. Two
pterodactyls soar
through a painted
sky punctuated
by tremendous smoke-
rings from a volcano.
      Beyond this hall
the Ice Age glitters
faintly--then human
steps inscribed in
glaciers, slopes
of frozen artifacts
floating on exhibit...

What chills the blood
is not the reconstructed
remnants of a reptile
eons dead but a word
buried in the head,
its connotations
glimmer like swirling
grains of dust. *Extinction.*
How easily our flesh
will vanish, our bodies
reveal what they've
always kept hid--
the intricate intersect
of bone, the oblique
geometry of the extinct.

I like this alot cool way to look
at the inevitability of human extinction

Landscape with Querulous Couple *Funny title*

They were returning
from somewhere--
just the two of them
arguing in the car--
one wants to stop
at a motel for the night;

This is my girlfriend

the other, who is driving,
wants to continue along
the mapped-out route

This is me

they've followed.
No stopovers.
No detours.
They are not lovers;
though one longs to be,
the other fears
a life beyond the
certainty of roadmaps.
Accusations. Denials.
Miles of deepening silence.
Till one lights a cigarette
& coughs. The other watches
the moon--red as a burning
tire--wobble over the highway.
The sky laden with stars,
faint & non-negotiable.

reminds me of when I drove to myrtle beach with my girlfriend except we both love eachother

After the Summer

My neighbor's garden is dying: all the tended flowerbeds
strewn with debris, the sumptuous rose that flamed
through August withers on its scaffold of thorns.
By the fence sunflowers droop, their faces tattered,
their shadows thin like the shadows of the ravished,
the full-blown, in lonely hospices. Maples shed their leaves
in fevered heaps; summer trees--frail and gray--
mock us with winter gestures. Soon the pond will
freeze over and reflect the sun as a glimmering
point--the way the eyes of the dead are said
to retain a last dwindling speck of light...
I'm thinking how my neighbor Walter, who tested
positive last March, chose to plant and cultivate,
chose to nurture such vulnerable, transitory blooms.
I marvel at his steadfastness, his willingness to confront
recurrent wastage. Next spring when the world emerges
from the last snowfall and the warm light hovers
I'll see him--if he's here--working on his knees,
his head bowed, his hands moving in the deep earth.

Very nice connection to the frailty
of flowers and the frailty of human
life. Perhaps his neighbor plants them because
he has control of their life even if for a
short while.

Disappearing

The honeybees are leaving us,
disappearing from our world

Mornings, they swarm
to work, like us;
evenings so
few return

They offer no explanations,
forward no goodbye notes

Their empty hives erupt with silence...

We look away
No time to send search parties,
no time for rescue missions

The honeybees are leaving us

a mystery, dark as combs
of honey, a taste of doom
upon our tongues

The endangerment of honeybees is
going to be a huge problem in the future.
It is sad that they live without ever
really having an identity.

hongxiu

2011.

Mourning Dove

For days she presided
over the two perfect eggs

hidden in the boston fern
    hanging on the balcony.

    It rained all week;
her body's warmth

kept the nest dry,
    wings spread like tents.

    She'd nibble bread
chunks moist with jam,

but left the fern only
    when spelled by her mate.

    The rain stopped
in the night. Next morning

the balcony lay pillaged:
    flower boxes disheveled,

    pots overturned, soil
like dried blood scattered

across green carpet--the nest
  violated, bits of feather

  and broken shell, the dove
driven off most likely

by a squirrel.
  Hours later, one egg found

  behind a planter, its side
cracked open, its song escaped...

A tiny orange claw oozed
  out, so desperate to grip

  the world, to live in its
beautiful, ruthless light.

this poem is like the story of
Pandora's box how amongst all
the chaos a little glimmer of hope
let out a feeble yelp and emerged from
the box, weak but still present

The Sunfish

flaps across the pier's
dark, splintered wood

perfectly miming a scream.
Fishing lines awry,

two drunks grin and
chuckle a cruel toast:

Make it one for my baby and...
splashing beer on the shape

that twists at their feet.
The sun, an inflamed fish's

eye, pours its scalding
gaze over the water until

something like the river's
current surges through him,

and the boy, though fearful,
shoves past them and lifts

the sunfish in his palm,
as he would any soft

hapless thing, tosses
it back in the water.

Too scared
to be brave, yet somehow

he feels the world a little
less lost and themselves,

even the drunks,
a little less damned.

#1   encarnacion is truly a romantic
style poet, many of his work has
given human qualities to nature and vice
versa. It is abundantly clear his profound
respect for the natural world.

The Diving Bell

We're locked inside
a crowded metal
shell hunkered
deep in the gray
Atlantic. I hunger
for the exotic, expect
the silver blur
of sharks with ivory
teeth. No dice.
We see no fish,
no plants, only
the dead sheen
of saltwater. At last
the bell begins
its rise toward
the floating
light...

30 years later
we surface
in a hushed white
room; nurses like
angelfish stream
past the bed

where you
struggle behind
a respirator
mask. I listen
to your breaths
ebb farther
apart, imagine
a bell--stranger
than the one
we once rode--
drawing the sick
up out of their
deathbeds
to enter
its chamber
of amber sea-
light. Here are
fathoms of cold
sunken gloom.
A shadow flickers.
A sleek fin circles
the room.

The idea of the bell is both unsettling and encouraging as it becons you to death ultimately, but not permanent death by any means.

Winter Light
(for my mother)

You're gone.

The severance seems almost surgical:
quick, deft, no loose ends. The phone
rings, a nurse's voice breaks the news.

Our insufficient grief... ⌐Sometimes when we lose
someone it's hard to feel anything⌐

I want something dramatic:
calamities of such proportion
they'll tear the earth apart.

Snow falls quietly.

The first moment we see you dead
an immense absence begins
to insinuate itself. I feel

the cool stiffening flesh

of your body in the hospital
bed and think, *this is fact,*
hard irrevocable fact

On the window sill

yellow chrysanthemums bloom
in the flared green vase,
unperturbed by the occasion.

Outside, streets whiten

in the winter light, wind stirs
the bones of naked trees,
footprints, clear and stark,

fill again with snow.

This poem is really sad. The end
is so depressing but beautiful, and
winter the perfect metaphor for death.

Saying the Names

Today I visit the graves of my family,
so many lost to the world of light.
Yet so long as I come here
they've not entirely vanished:
the bodies that the earth's reclaimed
are dross; spirits live beyond
expired flesh. I feel presence
in their hovering absence;
a little faith in the imagination
and they shimmer with all the light
beyond the grave. I bow my head,
walk from stone to stone,
murmuring each chiseled name.

It is obvious he believes in
something after death. How true the
presence of something at the graves of
loved ones, and how grounding it is to
be there and realize you will be there
someday devoid of consciousness.

Abandoned Graveyard

Look alive once you've climbed
the torn wire fence, crossed
the damaged footbridge joining
together these littered, weed-
tangled banks; no serious
mood will concede this foul
flow's a creek. Watch
for tumbled headstones,
for patches of grass
with the green tread out,
watch for shards of glass
where the mock orange flamed.
                    Near a path
ground with butts overflowing
like an ashtray, a blue sedan,
minus wheels, blisters beneath
the matchhead of sun.
It's home for someone whose
address is the NO DUMPING
sign, who gardens in rubbish,
scolds the loud crows,
claims the dead as her kin.

This deserted old woman
--Our Lady of Squalor--
sifts through piles
of smoldering trash,
as if to retrieve
all we've forgotten,
accidentally discarded,
irrevocably lost.

This gives a different feel to the abandoned graveyard. I find them most unsettling

"Night Shadows"
(Edward Hopper, etching on paper, 1921)

Somewhere in the middle
of the night, someone
is watching a man walk
down an empty street,
past dark buildings,
a closed cigar store.
Someone hovers, unseen,
above the sidewalk,
listens to footsteps
strike the cold cement.
Who is the man? Where
is he going? Why
the late hour, the long
overcoat and fedora?
Is he pursued?
Viewed from this height,
this peculiar angle,
he seems perhaps
another immigrant,
burdened with such
anonymity, his shoes
sink though the crust
of shadow on the ground.
He's drawn toward
a light that emanates
from a source beyond
the dim etched scene,

Is he a ghost. That
is the impression that
I get.

a light that conspires
with cross-hatched lines
to insinuate somehow
a dank, yellow gloom.
But what's the long
ominous shaft falling
obliquely across his path?
The shadow of a street-
light? A chasm widening
until he's swallowed?
The corner hydrant
takes no notice, and the watcher--
perhaps a blonde
naked in starlight
or a man etching
with beautiful hands--
turns from the dark
window as wind
hisses through
a crack in one corner
of the pane.

This is an awesome poem the imagery is so vibrant.

Tiara and the Calla Lilies

She'd slip into the diner
  just before we closed.
"Hey, girl!"
  waitresses shouted,
cooks winked.
    We knew that sultry
smile, knew the way
  it paid her bills.
Once a guy cuffed her
  to his bed, held a Bic
to her nipple until
  flesh seared; twice
he paid her good
  money to talk dirty
at the art museum.
    "No, really,
the dude was weird!"
  She whispered
obscenities while
  he stared
at the naked body
  of a girl
worshipping calla lilies...
  Now she's vanished.
Days pass. Months.

[handwritten annotation: Some people have a certain quality to them the french have a word for it]

Maybe one night
we'll see her on a corner,
   clothes disheveled,
hair a nightmare
   of tangles.
We'll call "Tiara,"
   but she'll hear
only wind careen
   off the river; we'll wave
but she will stare
   through us and see
only steam hissing
   from a street vent,
beneath a moon
   white as the flowers
in Diego Rivera's —
   great painting
"Nude with Calla Lilies."

he is describing the painting and
giving it a life, and backstory. This is
an interesting concept.

Bulosan Listens to
a Recording of Robert Johnson

You sing a hard blues,
black man. You too have been driven:
a tumbleweed in harsh wind.
I close my eyes, your voice rolls
out of the delta, sliding
over flashy chords
that clang like railroad tracks.

Gotta keep movin'
Gotta keep movin'
Blues fallin' down like hail

One summer
I worked the *wash-lye*
section of a cannery up north,
scrubbed schools of headless fish,
breathed ammonia fumes so fierce
I almost floated off
like the arm of a friend,
chopped clean at the elbow
by a cutter's machine.

Gotta keep movin'
Gotta keep movin'
Hellhound on my trail

We are the lost men, *kaibigan,*
our pockets empty of promise.
Mississippi/California--
bad luck conspires against us,
cheap wine stings in our veins.
We reel drunk and bitter
under the white, legal sun.
Robert Johnson/Carlos Bulosan--
our names so different,
our song the same.

They say Robert Johnson sold his soul
to the devil, the way that man played guitar
I wouldn't be surprised if he did

Summer of LOVE, an Elegy

"The bells from the schools of war
will be ringing"--A.L

Arthur Lee, when I listen
to *Forever Changes*, it's 1967.
I imagine my hair long,
my bell-bottoms snug but still fitting.
I play a vinyl copy
of your album, trying
to keep your death secret
from those songs. But
the news today will be
the movies for tomorrow.
I burn a fresh cone
of jasmine & clear my mind
of everything as smoke swirls
around the last butterfly
mobile I've saved from the
'60s--its tattered wings
still aflutter in even
the faintest wind.

The passing of time can feel like an
instant. It's things like the jasmine or
the song that are for lack of a better
expression a time machine transporting us back
to a place so familiar

Surf City

The summer I saw Jan & Dean
perform "Surf City"
on American Bandstand
I practiced in the tight   *resonant   particulars*
collarless suit I bought
from Slacs 'N' Jacs',
envisioned my name engraved
on golden platters
spinning endlessly
in the starlit Hall of Fame.
O, tall blond America: — *Nice*
I was short
and swarthy, obscure
as the flip side
of most pop 45s.
Two girls for every boy,
they sang. But I couldn't--
my voice flat, my ears
clogged with dissonance.
            Still, sometimes
I imagined finding that
perfect wave, rising as
if from prayer, veering
off in miracles of balance--
my black hair streaming,
my surf board shining,
eclipsing the sun.

The Fabulous Diving Horse
Today at Noon!

Remember Crysta
  and her diving horse,
Sea Squire?

Once, as a child, I sat
  in the bleachers
at a famous seaside pier

watching a woman
  on a foam-white horse
wave to the crowd

from a platform
  high in the air.
How the sequins

on her swimsuit
  glittered like flecks
of light on water;

how the drumroll
  built toward the
inevitable:

each of us gazing
 upward with
suspended breath,

the noon sun bright
 as any spotlight,
until the sudden

flight of woman
 and horse--
the leap of faith

we all took together.
 Remember that
moment's rapture--

the dazed and
 the dazzling--
how they splashed down,

 how the ovation rose?

I'm not big on the illustrations
they seem a bit rushed. This poem is a bit
to straight forward

48

My Cat and I Sit Out on the Balcony
After Dinner, Watching the Sunset
and Pretending We're Famous Poets

I feel like Cavafy done with another day's
tedium, proofreading letters in English
at his Irrigation Office, Alexandria, 1911--

except I've spent my day in New Jersey
a century later, engaged in the equally
tedious task of editing MARC records.

Moon reminds me of Li Po as she sits
quietly staring at nothing while the crickets
gather, rehearsing their evening song.

She's "dwelling in the moment," as my Buddhist
buddy would say, and I envy the ease with which
she's free of the ten thousand stressful things.

"Little Li Po," I whisper. She turns
her head, stifles a yawn, gives me a look
of infinite patience, as if to say: *Li Po?*

Oh, Please. Get real--hello???
We return to our own meditations;
the sun floats above us like a red pavilion

on a mountain somewhere in Szechwan, 760 A.D.,
old monks, sure-footed as cats, climbing paths
toward the painted clouds and waterfalls.

I too have sat outside with my cat and
I imagined we were sharing a moment together.
Called her the reincarnation of george harrison

49

Shark Roping

(In magic rituals certain Solomon Islanders
hunt sharks with ropes, clubs, incantations)

In the islands
   in the coral light
      of dawn, a man
paddles out from shore;
   his outrigger glides
      above the sunken
bar, the schools
   of iridescent fish.
      Sun skitters
across the waves.
   His back quivers
      in the wind.
He mouths a chant,
   scrapes the rattle
      made from purple
coconut shell
   against the scarred hull.
      Fish scatter
like shards of glass.
   His racket lures
      the reef shark--

emissary of grace
   and terror--up from
      the bluer depths;
it circles once,
   the dorsal fin
      sleek with malice.
Caught in the
   dangling noose, it's
      yanked to the surface.
Now water churns
   with the shark's mute
      wrath. But the islander,
this chanter of magic,
   grips the rope, wields
      the club, claims the beast
by endurance, by patience.
   He lives the dazzling art
      of balance out where glare
obliterates the horizon.

Sharks scare the living shit out of me
their eyes are so lifeless like a dolls
eyes

Cavafy Online

Surfing the Net
I found Cafe Cavafy:
dark, digital taverna,
virtual replica of
those bars you prowled
in Alexandria a century
of midnights ago. Enlarged,
the screen lit up
a stage, frozen figures,
a button that clicked
on bouzouki music.
                    Suddenly
I was at the table
next to yours
watching the handsome
young man extract himself
from the shadows,
pause shyly beside
you a moment,
whisper and vanish.

Where he went
that night in 1910
is anybody's guess,

but you, Cavafy,
walked slowly
along Rue Lipsius
to your flat,
already haunted
by his absence,
by the moon's
dark, forbidden face.

1910?

Moon Tree

--sycamore planted from seed carried to the moon by
astronaut Stuart A. Roosa
on Apollo XIV

How ordinary the tree appears: its thin dappled trunk,
few scratched initials, skeletal branches stark in the wind.
Dwarfed by the
park's older trees Roosa's sycamore feigns irrelevance,
all promise of green leaves on this March afternoon--illusory.
How deceptive things can seem: think of those who grow
among us
day after day distinguished by no discernible sign,
imbued with nothing otherworldly.
Yet consider how
one day they may
rise, full bloom,
out of ordinary lives
to renew our belief
in the extraordinary,
to transform our world,
this minor sphere
whirling in dark
fathoms of space--
its perfect pearl of a moon.

beautiful imagery

54

"I Wonder How Long the Night Will Last"

I stand alone with ten thousand sorrows
Tu Fu

Some nights stressed out--
knots grinding in my gut,
fists clenching, unclenching--
I need a little help but refuse
my former drug of choice,
shots of vodka never faze me,
even forbidden sex can't tease
a spark. I drive miles of moonlight
to reach the Perkiomen,
forgetting ten thousand sorrows
along the way, free to hook-up
(if only in my mind) with Princess
Le-Chang, dead some 1400 years,
who might share a cup of wine,
a little weed, & ask what light
floats on darkness tonight.
We can stare a long time
at the river, praise the moon's
thumbprint on water,
its bright & healing touch.

Some night, you just know you will
never forget and they do last forever, that is
at least for the longevity of your life

55

Acknowledgments

"The Snake Plant" appeared in *Asian America*

"The Diving Bell" appeared in *Grasslands Review*

"Mourning Dove" appeared in *The Hurricane Review*

"Bulosan Listens to a Recording of Robert Johnson" appeared in *The Indiana Review*

"After the Summer" appeared in *The Paterson Literary Review*

"August," "Express" and "The Fabulous Diving Horse Today at Noon" appeared in *The Sabal Palm Review*

"Tiara and the Calla Lilies" appeared in *Tobeco Literary & Artistic Journal*

"Bulosan Listens to a Recording of Robert Johnson" was reprinted in the following anthologies: *Blues Poem, Letters to America, The Open Boat: Poems from Asian America,* and *Unsettling America*

Alfred Encarnacion has been employed as a caterer, teacher, librarian, and media specialist. He holds degrees from Clarion University and Temple University where he taught in the English Department for seven years. His poems have appeared in national journals--such as *Florida Review, Indiana Review, North American Review,* and *The Paterson Literary Review*-- and have been anthologized in *Identity Lessons, Letters to America, The Open Boat: Poems from Asian America, and Unsettling America.* This is his first collection of poetry.

"Of sorrows, Alfred Encarnacion says, 'Given the right imagination/they convert into capital.' In *The Outskirts of Karma,* we have the right imagination. This is a wise and beautiful book that helps us to live in a world of 'beautiful, ruthless light.'"

--Chris Bursk

Hong Xia has had an eclectic career as a physician, teacher, production director, fashion designer, and, most emphatically, an artist. The striking originality of her work perhaps stems from the fact that she is "self-taught," an artist who eschews any particular style in favor of a belief in the transforming power of the imagination to create the appropriate forms for her art. She is inspired by the emotionality that can be derived from objects, scenes, or situations, and her art rests in its ability to manifest "moments of memory" that the viewer can share with her. In her work she, like T. S. Eliot, attempts to discover the "objective correlative" for her emotional response to stimuli.

Hong Xia's Chinese watercolors have appeared in numerous group exhibitions, and her fashion designs--which have been published--have won local and national awards. Her recent discovery of painting on glass and china has added a new dimension to her work. This is her first collaboration with a poet.